Original title:
The Intergalactic Poet

Copyright © 2025 Creative Arts Management OÜ
All rights reserved.

Author: Juliana Wentworth
ISBN HARDBACK: 978-1-80567-810-6
ISBN PAPERBACK: 978-1-80567-931-8

Galactic Rhythms of Time

In a spaceship made of gum,
Space cows chew and hum.
Each twinkle is a tune,
As we dance around the moon.

Stars wear hats, and laugh like kids,
Comets fly with silly jigs.
Galaxies spin in a goofy way,
Making every night feel like play.

Tales of Life Among the Stars

A martian works at a cosmic diner,
Serving space milkshakes with a whiner.
UFOs zoom in for a bite,
While astronauts bobble in delight.

Aliens trade their favorite snacks,
Green donuts, pink chips in glowing packs.
Their stories weave through time and light,
A buffet of laughter, pure delight.

Reflections on an Infinite Canvas

Nebulae paint with colors bright,
Swirling giggles in the starry night.
Psychedelic dreams upon a sky,
Where robots and aliens munch and sigh.

Paintbrushes made of cosmic dust,
Create a universe that's a must!
Laughter echoes through the void,
Making boredom utterly destroyed.

Sonnet of the Solar Winds

Solar winds with a playful jest,
Tickle the planets, making them rest.
Jupiter spins in polka-dot glee,
As Saturn's rings giggle, "Look at me!"

Asteroids roll with a clumsy flair,
While rocket ships play tag without a care.
In this cosmic circus, joy abounds,
As laughter rings across all the bounds.

Fragments of a Cosmic Diary

In a starship made of cheese,
I wrote my dreams with ease,
Gravity forgot my name,
Chasing comets was my game.

Martians danced in polka dots,
While Jupiter brewed coffee pots,
Saturn wore a hula hoop,
And Pluto started a dance troupe.

Celestial Ballads of Lost Worlds

A singing asteroid passed by,
It crooned a tune to the sky,
Venus tried to join the fun,
But tangled in her own hot sun.

Black holes have a wicked grin,
They pull you in, you can't win,
With funny hats they spin around,
While galaxies try to break ground.

Rhymes from the Milky Way

A comet's tail was quite the sight,
It flicked and flared like a light,
Stars whispered secrets to the night,
While aliens held a friendly fight.

In a nebula, I found my muse,
It danced in colors, bright hues,
With giggles floating on the breeze,
It told the universe to please!

Galactic Harmonies

Sing, oh planets, in bright bands,
Play your tunes with cosmic hands,
Mars strummed a guitar quite sweet,
 While Pluto tapped its tiny feet.

A lunar rabbit hopped with flair,
It twirled around with zero care,
The Milky Way held a late-night show,
Where even asteroids had room to glow.

Astral Wordscarves

In universe's closet, scarves swirl,
Made of stardust, they twirl and whirl.
Each thread a pun, a cosmic joke,
It's fashion week in a black hole smoke.

Comets wear ties, supernovas sport hats,
Alien models strut on space-mice mats.
Glistening in twilight, they prance and pose,
While galaxies giggle at their dazzling clothes.

Luminous Letters Across Space

Letters zoom from planet to star,
Puns that bounce, oh how they spar!
A B from Andromeda, a C from the Moon,
They join in the dance, a cosmic cartoon.

With ink made of starlight, they scribble a song,
Giggles echoing where they all belong.
Silly stanzas float like balloons in the night,
Chasing meteors, spreading delight.

Dancing with Cosmic Shadows

Shadows jiggle on Mercury's gleam,
Flickering to the interstellar dream.
Saturn's rings chuckle, they spin in delight,
Conducting a waltz under blue starlit night.

Nebulas twist in a comical spree,
Wobbling together, too funny to see.
Black holes spin tales, quirks in the dark,
While quasars laugh, igniting a spark.

Celestial Canvas of Aspirations

In the void, a canvas stretched wide,
With paint made of wishes, stars bonafide.
Doodles of dreams float in bright hues,
Each stroke a giggle, a cosmos amuse.

Aliens sketching with laughter and glee,
Creating a mural for all eyes to see.
With whirls and swirls, their colors collide,
In this whimsical universe, joy cannot hide.

Nebulae and Nostalgia

In a starry cafe, I sipped my tea,
Watching black holes do the cha-cha, you see.
Nebulae dance in a glittery swirl,
While comets argue over who's the best girl.

An astronaut missed his launch again,
Blaming it all on that pesky zen pen.
I laughed so hard, spilled my cosmic brew,
As planets giggled in the midnight dew.

Echoes in the Void

Rockets zoom past, with quirky tunes,
While space dust plays chess with the moons.
An alien poet spills ink on Mars,
Writing sonnets about Venus' bazaars.

The vacuum complained of a lack of laughs,
As meteors juggled with gravity's gaffes.
Unicorns pranced on a Saturn-ring,
And Jupiter chuckled at the chaos they'd bring.

Cosmic Ink and Celestial Dreams

With a quill made of stardust, I write my rhymes,
On a galaxy's parchment, in whimsical times.
Black holes wear glasses, read books upside down,
While my spaceship joyrides through a cosmic town.

Every star is a wish that forgot how to fly,
As nebulae giggle and twinkle nearby.
Celestial dreams bounce in playful glee,
While planets coordinate a grand jubilee.

Lyrical Journeys Through Time

Time travelers stumble over rhyme and reason,
Mixing up epochs like a jigsaw season.
Aliens tap dance on a timeline spree,
While history winks at a pun, just for free.

With a cosmic flute, I lead a parade,
Of quirky astronauts who've somehow strayed.
They're lost in lyrics, traveling through light,
Creating laughter in the depths of the night.

Odyssey of Words through the Universe

In a spaceship made of rhymes,
We sail through galactic times.
Stars wink as we craft each phrase,
While nebulae dance in poetic haze.

Quasars giggle, black holes chuckle,
As our verses spin with a subtle smuggle.
We scribble sonnets on comet tails,
And send love notes on asteroid trails.

In the Realm of Cosmic Poetry

On a planet where puns take flight,
Comets race in pure delight.
Vacuum grips, but we don't care,
In zero-G, we float and share.

Alien jokers play with words,
Silly stanzas fly like birds.
Gravity laughs at our silly schemes,
As we weave tales from our dreams.

Chronicles of Celestial Wanderers

We journey through the stardust bright,
With laughter echoing through the night.
Meteor showers rain down jokes,
While quirky aliens crack their hoax.

In space, the punchlines bloom and swell,
As planets giggle, oh do tell!
Each rhyme we throw becomes a star,
And we bask in our cosmic bazaar.

Metaphors from the Starship

Our starship's fueled by silly dreams,
With metaphors that burst at the seams.
Time travel's just a wordy game,
As we prank the universe with our name.

Asteroids roll with laughter loud,
While starlights gather, forming crowds.
We scribble joy on solar flares,
And dance with the cosmos—no cares!

Time's Celestial Metronome

In a cosmos where time takes a dance,
Stars twirl around in their sparkly pants.
Jupiter giggles with each tick and tock,
While asteroids play hopscotch on the block.

Planets spin tales of their perplexing fate,
Saturn's rings wobbly, can't quite relate.
Lightyears away, they still crack a grin,
As comets join in for a bit of a spin.

Neptune laughs heartily with a deep sea sound,
Echoing laughter that swings all around.
In the heart of the void, such joy does sprout,
As the universe winks and gives a shout.

Each moment they share, bizarre yet sublime,
Makes every tick-tock feel like rhyme over rhyme.

Celestial Imaginations and Cosmic Dreams

In a nebula's cradle, dreams find their shape,
Galaxies giggle and take a long gape.
With wishes like stardust, they twinkle and tease,
Creating a cosmos that's sure to please.

Mars paints a picture with ketchup and fries,
While Venus attempts to bake sweet moon pies.
Cosmic imaginations twirling in flight,
Each star a giggle that shines through the night.

Black holes hold secrets, but with a sly wink,
They swirl like dervishes, more fun than you think.
Quasars burst laughter, bright beams from afar,
Each lightyear a chuckle, a cosmic bizarre.

In the grand theater where planets all scheme,
They dream up adventures in a fanciful dream.

The Song of Distant Suns

Far off in the sky, where the suns set ablaze,
They gather in circles, performing their plays.
With solar flares twinkling, they sing out a cheer,
While meteors join in with a hot, fiery sphere.

A distant sun hums a tune full of flair,
And the comets, with style, flip through the air.
Neutron stars bang on a cosmic old drum,
While galaxies join in, each strum a big 'yum.'

Light-years apart yet still close in their fun,
They toast with starlight, their laughter begun.
In the echoes of space, such harmony flows,
A symphony written in radiant prose.

So listen real close to the sound of the skies,
Where solar orchestras make spirits arise.

Lifted by Galactic Winds

Floating through space on a whimsical breeze,
Stardust and laughter swirl with such ease.
The Milky Way tickles as comets all glide,
Riding the currents like surf on the tide.

Saturn's rings spiral, creating a dance,
Galactic winds whirl, giving stars a chance.
Orbs of wild colors, all giggling in flight,
As cosmic balloons drift by day and by night.

Planets chuckle, exchanging their jests,
While the sun gives a wink, with rays that are blessed.
Each breeze, a whisper, a playful delight,
Soaring through realms where the laughter takes flight.

In cosmic playgrounds, with joy there's no end,
Lifted by winds where the galaxies blend.

Gravity's Unwritten Verses

In a galaxy where apples float,
I wrote a poem on a little boat.
Stars giggle as they twinkle bright,
While I scribble lines in the dead of night.

Planets dance in a merry throng,
Singing silly tunes, nothing wrong.
Saturn laughs with rings so wide,
As I trip on cosmic waves, my pride.

Asteroids tumble and roll with glee,
Chasing my thoughts like a puppy can spree.
Comets join in, tails all ablaze,
It's a carnival of words, a merry maze.

So, if you see me spinning around,
It's just gravity's poetry doing its rounds.
I'll catch a rhyme before it flies,
In this silly universe that never lies.

Reaching for Comets in Rhyme

With a lasso made of cosmic dust,
I chase comets, in humor, I trust.
They giggle at my awkward stance,
As they swirl and twirl in a playful dance.

Nebulae chuckle, their colors bright,
Painting the dark with a comedy light.
I reach for stars with my hands so wide,
But they bounce back, as if they hide.

"Catch me if you can," a comet sings,
As I wobble like I've boundless springs.
Planets roll over in fits of laughter,
While I scribble rhymes, forever after.

So on this ride through the cosmic fun,
I'll jot down jokes till my day is done.
In the tapestry of the space-time chime,
I'll keep on reaching, just for the rhyme.

Luna's Lament and the Cosmic Wail

Oh Luna weeps in silvery light,
Her tears fall down in the starry night.
But hold on tight, let's not despair,
Her puddles are craters, a dance affair.

She wails of love lost to a sunbeam,
As meteors mock her with a bright gleam.
"Why so sad?" asks a passing star,
"Join in the fun; it's not very far!"

In her fabled tales of lunar plight,
There's always room for a giggle or fright.
Cosmic chuckles mingle with her sighs,
As I jot down verses, beneath the skies.

So wipe those tears, dear Luna moon,
Let's rhyme and dance to a silly tune.
For even in sorrow, a laugh will prevail,
In the heart of the night, hear the cosmic wail.

Orbiting Emotions in Stardust

In the orbits of feelings, I spin and sway,
Emotions like rockets launching all day.
Joy zooms past with a whoosh and a cheer,
While sadness drifts slowly, but never near.

A black hole giggles, swallowing tears,
While love asteroids bounce through my fears.
I juggle with laughter, juggling with glee,
In this cosmic circus, come laugh with me!

Gravitational pull keeps pulling me tight,
Through laughter and gaffes, I take flight.
Neptune whispers a joke so absurd,
As I chuckle on high, lost in every word.

So let's orbit together, and spin like confetti,
In stardust and joy, our memories steady.
A galaxy of giggles is all we require,
In this universe of dreams, we'll never tire.

Cosmic Elegies Under Shooting Stars

In a galaxy far where the aliens dine,
They ponder the rhythms of space and of time.
With forks made of stardust and spoons of pure light,
They feast on the comets, a cosmic delight.

The black holes are laughing, they spin and they twirl,
While planets join in for a cosmic whirl.
A nebula's giggle floats out in the breeze,
As stars share their jokes with the swaying green trees.

In meteor showers, the wishes collide,
Hoping one day, they'll take a fun ride.
Aliens chase with their tails up in glee,
Writing funny poems on Orions' back spree.

So if you look up with a twinkle tonight,
Remember that laughter is floating in light.
For in this vast ether, all's playful and bright,
Cosmic elegies dance 'neath the shooting stars' flight.

A Tapestry of Cosmic Verse

Knitted in starlight, the cosmos unfolds,
With patterns of giggles that nobody told.
Galaxies churn like a whimsical stew,
And meteors sing silly songs just for you.

The comets get tangled in yarn made of dreams,
Weaving their tales with astronomical beams.
In Saturn's ring circus, the clowns tumble down,
While Jupiter chuckles, a jovial crown.

Each black hole's a joker with infinite space,
Who swallows your worries, then gives them a chase.
Quasars are pranksters, they flash and they beam,
Creating confusion, a cosmic theme.

So wrap up your laughter in blankets of night,
Count stars like sheep while you join in the flight.
For woven in whispers of cosmic perverse,
Is an ode to the joy of a tapestry's verse.

Celestial Melodies in the Dark

Out in the void where the sound waves do dance,
Celestial singers have taken a chance.
With guitars made of starlight, they strum through the night,
While comets clap hands in a jubilant flight.

The moon joins the party, she croons out a tune,
While planets all sway to a cosmic cartoon.
The stars keep the beat with their twinkling delight,
Creating a symphony, sparkling and bright.

A supernova bursts like a laugh in the dark,
Sending echoes of joy on a cosmic lark.
Uranus winks playfully as he hops,
While asteroids drum with their bumpy little tops.

So lean back and listen, let laughter abound,
For in cosmic music, happiness is found.
In the silence of space where the wonders embark,
Playful melodies twinkle in the dark.

Astral Reflections and Rhythms

Mirrors in space show a funny sight,
Where shadows are giggling, and stars take flight.
Eclipses are just if the sun blinks too hard,
A moment of chuckles, an astral façade.

Pluto throws parties with ice cream galore,
While quirky little satellites dance on the floor.
They slide through the cosmos in a merry parade,
And all of the starlings in unison played.

The asteroids tumble, doing flips and spins,
While meteorites giggle, "Oh, let the fun begin!"
Hubble's peering out with a spark in his eye,
Sharing tales of the cosmos, oh my, oh my!

So join in this dance of celestial cheer,
Where laughter and joy echo loud and clear.
For in all the reflections of cosmic delight,
Are rhythms of humor shining ever so bright.

Poetic Orbits of Celestial Bodies

In a galaxy full of rhyme,
Planets dance without a chime.
Stars giggle in the velvety night,
Winking at comets taking flight.

Asteroids rolling in carefree glee,
Throwing space parties, wild and free.
Moonbeams play hide and seek,
As rockets chase with a cheeky squeak.

Black holes whisper jokes quite sly,
While Neptune rolls its eye up high.
In cosmic cafes, aliens sip tea,
Sharing tales of their wild spree.

Quasars beam with flashing lights,
Telling puns of starry nights.
Eclipses giggle, dimming the sun,
As the universe joins in on the fun.

Beyond Horizons of Dream and Thought

Beneath a veil of dreams so wide,
A space cat takes a wondrous ride.
Jupiter's moons join in the chase,
Chasing stardust all over the place.

A comet's tail is a feathered plume,
Tickling the stars, bright with bloom.
Nebulae blend in colors so bright,
Painting the cosmos with sheer delight.

Fairies of space whisper tunes,
While asteroids tap dance like loons.
Galactic squirrels jump from star to star,
Collecting nuts from planets afar.

Beyond the void of strange black holes,
Banter echoes, leaving giggling souls.
On astral swings, they twist and twirl,
Creating chaos in a cosmic whirl.

The Silence Between Star Systems

In the hush of space, laughter brews,
Asteroids gossip like busy crews.
Nova bursts make quite a scene,
Spilling secrets from sights unseen.

Between the stars, shadows abound,
With echoes of chuckles all around.
Saturn's rings offer a playful ride,
While meteor showers take us for a glide.

Solar winds sing a breezy tune,
While aliens dance to the beat of the moon.
Quirky rockets glide with ease,
Whizzing past planets, much like a breeze.

Stars poke fun at time's cruel play,
Cosmic calendars flip every day.
In silence, there's laughter, a joyous flow,
In this vastness, we find our show.

Cosmic Chronicles of the Soul

In the great expanse where dreams collide,
Galaxies challenge the cosmic tide.
With quarks and leptons forming a song,
The universe hums, nothing feels wrong.

A whimsical tale of astral grace,
Starlit humor fills every space.
Comets plotting their playful schemes,
Woven in threads of colorful dreams.

Hyperdrive laughter fills the air,
While meteors race with style and flair.
Eons dance in a joyful spree,
Spinning yarns from infinity.

Wormholes twist and turn with glee,
Opening doors to what can't be.
Cosmic stories, both funny and bold,
Unfold in the stars, forever retold.

Starlit Scribbles from Faraway Realms

In a galaxy far, far away,
Aliens write in disarray.
With ink from comets, they doodle and play,
Sending their messages in a whacky way.

Tiny green hands scribble lines,
Under moons that smell like limes.
Their sense of humor, a cosmic tease,
Tickles the stars with interstellar ease.

Black holes giggle, while planets spin,
Jokes about gravity, where no one can win.
Asteroids crash with a thundering clatter,
While space dust dances in a shimmering scatter.

So next time you gaze at the night so bright,
Remember the poets, hidden from sight.
They laugh among stars, on journeys untold,
Writing their tales in the cosmos, bold.

The Universe's Hidden Verse

Between the stars, words take flight,
Witty quips at the speed of light.
Galactic giggles echo through space,
As stardust dribbles in a rhyming race.

Zebras on Saturn with polka dot styles,
Write tips for travel in sassy smiles.
Their cosmic critique of Earth's boring air,
Hints that the grass might be better up there.

Neptune's sonnets bubble and fizz,
Squeaky lyrics, oh what a whiz!
Pluto rolls laughter in icy cold,
Sharing the funniest tales that were told.

When you look up at that velvet night,
Know a verse may fly past in pure delight.
For the universe chuckles beyond our sight,
In verses that burst, dancing with light.

Poems Written in Meteor Showers

When shooting stars streak across the sky,
Poets giggle and give it a try.
They catch the sparks in their little jars,
Composing limericks on celestial cars.

Comets parade with tails that glitter,
While scribes on asteroids happily twitter.
Their silly sonnets lit up in flames,
Make the cosmos embrace silly games.

Jokes from Jupiter bounce off the moons,
Celebrating with laughter, oh how it tunes!
Meteor showers become open mics,
Where cosmic comedians score with their spikes.

So if a flash lights up your night,
It might be a poet, brimming with light.
Writing their verses in brilliant delight,
Making the universe feel just right.

Wanderings Among Celestial Bodies

In a nebula park, poets play hopscotch,
With comets as lanes—oh what a botch!
The Martians sell ice cream made out of stars,
While aliens giggle in hovercraft cars.

With quarks and quirks, they write in the air,
Filling the cosmos with quirks to spare.
Black holes sing songs of holes in their pants,
As Saturn's rings spin in rhythmic dance.

The moon whispers puns to the glowing sun,
Creating a cosmic joke that's just too fun.
Uranus snickers, saying, "I'm the best!"
While Venus just giggles, reclining at rest.

So pack up your stardust, grab a quill,
Join the laughter that dances at will.
Among celestial bodies, humor unfurls,
Writing the silliest tales of our worlds.

Rhythms Beyond the Blue

In a galaxy far away, it sings,
Silly notes from alien beings.
Dancing comets in jitterbug shoes,
Under stars, they giggle and snooze.

Planets twirl in a cosmic dance,
With moonbeams weaving a freaky prance.
Green aliens stumble, trip, and fall,
Laughter echoes, a harmonious call.

Black holes hum with a jazzy beat,
While quarks and leptons tap their feet.
Meteorites throw a wild ball,
Spinning verses—catch them all!

Through the cosmos, such fun galore,
With every rhyme, we long for more.
Silly songs from the stars above,
Universal laughter—what a love!

Untold Tales from the Cosmic Womb

In the cradle of stars, stories dwell,
Whispered secrets in a galactic shell.
A wormhole yawns, tales cascade,
Of toaster wars that aliens made.

Asteroids bicker over who is best,
A veggied alien put it to test.
They race with comets, oh what a sight,
Screaming, "I'm faster!" through the night.

Celestial chefs bake quasar pies,
Shooting stars toss toppings—oh, the cries!
Each one flavors the universe wide,
With ingredients from the cosmic tide.

Black holes spin yarns, a timeless tease,
Wrapping moments like space-time cheese.
In the vast expanse, laughter won't cease,
Cosmic giggles that grant some peace!

Mars and the Metaphor

On rusty Mars, the rovers joke,
"Is that a rock or an alien cloak?"
They dance on dust with robotic flair,
Chasing shadows through the thin Martian air.

Red sand sifts through their metal hands,
As they make up poems about distant lands.
They ponder if aliens pay for a ticket,
To watch Martians spin like a spinning cricket.

The rocket scientists have wild dreams,
Of cosmic tea and interstellar schemes.
"Should we try some Martian stew?" they say,
"Let's add some moon cheese, hip-hip-hooray!"

As craters echo with laughter's sound,
The metaphors tumble, swirling around.
In the red dust, joy is unconfined,
A playful wink from the universe, we find.

Jupiters' Whispering Stanzas

Jupiter rumbles with jovial tunes,
Swirling gas clouds and ballooning balloons.
The Great Red Spot spins silly lines,
While moons giggle and tease like playful swines.

Funky vibes from the swirling storms,
Creating poetry in bizarre forms.
Saturn's rings roll their eyes and sway,
"Jupiter's rhymes? Let's join the play!"

Ninja comets sneak a peek,
At vibrant verses, oh so unique.
With a wink from Io, the mischief spreads,
As fun-loving stanzas dance in our heads.

In the realm of gas and gassy gas,
Where verses frolic, and time will pass.
Jupiter's laughter fills the void,
Giving each moment a giggle employed.

Interstellar Musings

In spaceships made of cheese and dreams,
Floating through cosmic streams,
With alien pals, we write in ink,
Of moonlit dances and stars that wink.

Jupiter's got a funky beat,
While Venus brings the tasty suite,
Pluto's waving from afar,
Saying, 'I'm still a superstar!'

Comets twirl with tails so bright,
Scribbling poems in the night,
Asteroids throw a rhyming bash,
All in the cosmic literary cache.

So gather round, my starry friends,
Let's write till our laughter blends,
For in this vast, wacky expanse,
Even the black holes love to dance!

The Universe's Lyricist

A quasar sings a joyous tune,
While Saturn spins under the moon,
With rings all shiny and quite grand,
He pens a ballad 'bout a rocky land.

Zipping past the Martian dust,
In a rhyming flow we trust,
With meteors casting witty lines,
We craft our verses 'til the sun shines.

Galaxies twirl in perfect rhyme,
Wishing we could pause all time,
But laughter echoes through the void,
Joy in the cosmos can't be destroyed.

Join us on this stellar ride,
With each new word, we'll glide and glide,
The universe grins, its heart alight,
As we pen our poems into the night!

Sonnets to the Stars

Oh, how the Milky Way does tease,
With chocolate rivers and minty trees,
The stars giggle in the cosmic swirl,
While planets spin, in joy they twirl.

A wink from Orion, a bow so sleek,
Whispers of cosmic hide-and-seek,
With each bright flash, they say 'Hello!'
Under their glow, we steal the show.

Black holes are shy, but what a sight,
Turning back poetry, it's outta sight!
We scribble our jokes on stardust shores,
Where laughter lingers and adventure soars.

So here's to the brilliance, the humor and fun,
Dancing through space, on the run,
With every quip, our spirits soar,
In this cosmic circus, we long for more!

Orbiting Words

Words like asteroids take flight,
Spinning stories in the night,
With galaxies bursting into cheer,
As gravitational puns appear.

A nebula shapes a funny face,
Laughing in its cotton candy space,
While space-time tickles our silly bone,
We write our verses in a twinkling tone.

Through meteor showers, we play catch,
As supernovas strike their match,
Crafting snippets that drift and sway,
In this cosmic word ballet.

So round and round, our thoughts collide,
On this interstellar joyride,
With cosmic quips, we dance and twine,
Crafting a universe that's simply divine!

Starlit Musings on Distant Planets

Beneath the twinkling skies, so bright,
Aliens dance in the pale moonlight.
They juggle comets, take a spin,
Laughing loud, let the fun begin!

On Mars, they sip their cosmic tea,
Chatting with rocks, it's quite the spree.
Venus sings with a voice so sweet,
Even giants sway to the beat!

Jupiter's storms hear the rhymes,
Swirling clouds, they laugh at times.
Saturn's rings play the kazoo,
As they bop along, just a few!

Oh, drifting far in this cosmic feast,
Dreams take flight, and they never cease.
With every wink of a starry glance,
Intergalactic folks join the dance!

Lyrical Waves of the Universe

Riding waves on a starlit tide,
Galactic surfers, what a ride!
Catch a beam, and spin around,
Laughter echoes, a joyful sound!

Neptune splashes with a grin,
While cosmic dolphins dive right in.
They flip and twirl, oh, what a show,
In this vast space, where wonders flow!

Shooting stars play tag in flight,
Racing past on a whimsic night.
Every burst brings cheers and yells,
While comets weave fantastic spells!

Through swirling galaxies in attire,
Each heartbeat feels like a cosmic choir.
Join the party, feel the thrill,
As the universe dances, time stands still!

Suns of Inspiration

Golden suns with goofy grins,
Shining bright, let the fun begin.
They tell us jokes in solar flares,
While space critters dance in pairs!

Sunny rays tickle the night,
Bursting forth in pure delight.
Planets giggle, stars join in,
What a cosmic party we're in!

A supernova bursts with glee,
As asteroids dance, one, two, three.
Beaming light, like it's the show,
Creating shadows, putting on a glow!

Chasing light upon a whim,
This solar bash, let spirits brim.
Round and round on this endless ride,
Leave your worries far outside!

Moons of Reflection

Round and round the moons revolve,
In mirrored pools, mysteries solve.
Their giggles echo through the night,
As they play with dreams, pure delight!

With every glance from afar,
They wink and nod like a shooting star.
Reflecting tales of lost romance,
Swirling stories in a cosmic dance!

Each crater shares a secret old,
Filled with laughter, tales unfold.
Moonbeams painting wishes bright,
While shadows curl in playful light!

In the calm, they softly hum,
Inviting others to join the fun.
So when you look up, don't despair,
For moons are there with a joyful flare!

Whispers of the Milky Way

In the corridors of cosmic flow,
Whispers travel, soft and slow.
Galaxies giggle, a twinkle in eyes,
As stardust sprinkles from the skies!

With every spiral, tales are spun,
Of adventures shared, and laughter won.
A comet passing with a wink,
Joins the party, no time to think!

Constellations in a playful jest,
Compete for the title of the best.
With each twirl, they share a wink,
Sending smiles across the brink!

The night unfolds in tales of lore,
Whispers dance forevermore.
In this cosmic hug, we all unite,
As laughter echoes through the night!

Stars Beneath My Quill

Inky pools of cosmic night,
I scribble tales of starry light.
My pen has flown to worlds afar,
And danced beneath a purple star.

Each comet's tail, a line I write,
Of aliens with two left feet,
They trip on moons and giggle loud,
In tiny ships, they form a crowd.

I write of planets made of cheese,
Where astronauts enjoy a sneeze.
With every line, I hear them cheer,
A cosmic laugh, so bright and clear.

So join my quill in merry flight,
As we traverse the endless night.
With every word, the stars align,
In giggles shared through space and time.

Cosmic Verses Across the Void

Across the void, my poems stroll,
In search of humor, that's the goal.
I found a Martian, quite absurd,
Who thought the stars were just for birds.

His rhyme scheme stuttered, and he tripped,
While cosmic jesters laughed and dipped.
I wrote of fruit that stocks the sun,
Banana comets just for fun!

A black hole hiccuped, and I shouted,
Reversed my thoughts, and then I doubted.
Did gravity sense my crazy quip?
Or just ignore my poet's slip?

Through cosmic waves, my verses twirl,
As nebulae begin to swirl.
In laughter's echo, wisdom grew,
The universe is fun, it's true!

Ink from Distant Worlds

With ink from worlds I've never seen,
I craft the quirkiest routine.
A space squid waltzes, what a sight!
His tentacles twirl, oh what delight!

Galactic puns on asteroids,
Where laughter blooms and fear avoids.
A neutron star's a cheeky fellow,
Who shines and glows, a cosmic yellow.

I penned a rhyme on Mars' fine dust,
Where rovers sand-surf, as they must.
An astronaut fell, did a spin,
And laughed aloud—what a winsome grin!

So let my ink, from far-off places,
Bring joy and laughter to your faces.
In every word, a galaxy's heart,
Where humor and starlight are never apart.

Celestial Stanzas in Space

In stanzas spun of starlit glee,
I write of spaceships made of tea.
With biscuits flying in their wake,
They traveled far, for friendship's sake.

A jovial quasar sings a tune,
That makes the planets sway and swoon.
I laughed with stars, they winked at me,
As gravity danced on light debris.

My ink drips stories from the moon,
Of cosmic critters prancing soon.
In comical tones, they all unite,
To share a giggle in the night.

So come, dear friend, let's take the leap,
Into this space where laughter's deep.
With every phrase, the cosmos beams,
In silly dreams, our starlight gleams.

Stars as Sentence Shapers

In the night, stars twinkle bright,
They're punctuation marks of pure delight.
Comets zoom, dashing with flair,
While planets giggle, floating in air.

Galaxies spin with a cosmic cheer,
Whispers of jokes from light-years near.
Black holes snicker, pulling things tight,
As meteors tumble, a dazzling sight.

Asteroids chuckle, bumping around,
With moons that waltz, oh, what a sound!
Saturn's rings, a glittering jest,
All in this verse, interstellar fest!

So grab your quill, let's write in space,
Where every laugh finds its own place.
With cosmic ink and a twinkling eye,
We'll pen our tales in the endless sky.

Threads of Infinity

Woven in starlight, laughter's thread,
Nebulas joking, we giggle instead.
Entangled in dreams, we spin and dance,
In the fabric of space, there's always a chance.

Jokes from the cosmos come whizzing by,
With asteroids laughing, oh my, oh my!
A supernova's pop, a burst of glee,
As the universe grins, so vast and free.

Cosmic yarns spun with whimsical flair,
Each twist and turn fills the void with air.
Galactic pun stars light up the void,
In this realm where boredom's destroyed.

So grab a thread, join the cosmic fun,
In the tapestry where laughter's begun.
With every stitch, let's weave and play,
A giggle in the Milky Way!

Verse from the Cosmic Sea

Waves of laughter crash on shores,
In the vastness where nonsense soars.
A tidal wave of silly glee,
Splashing about the cosmic sea.

Stars bobbing like buoys in the foam,
Planets paddling, far from home.
Galaxies whirl in a dance so spry,
As quarks giggle, floating by.

Cosmic fish tease with their finned grace,
Swirling and twirling in boundless space.
Laughter bubbles in every swirl,
As comets dive, giving a twirl.

So dip your toes in this playful brine,
Where the universe sings and stars align.
With every verse written in delight,
We'll sail through space on a giggling night!

Phrases from Parallel Universes

In a universe not quite like ours,
Words frolic freely, slipping through bars.
Jokes twinkle in dimensions unseen,
As puns take flight, spry and keen.

Cows in space with hats of cheese,
Sliding on rainbows, doing as they please.
Time loops back for another laugh,
While gravity tickles, bending the path.

Planets swing on the cosmic vine,
Sipping stardust, feeling divine.
Einstein's cat plays with quantum flair,
In a universe lively, beyond compare.

So let's ride the waves of humor's grace,
Through realms where laughter leaves a trace.
In these phrases, so strange and bright,
We'll find our joy, just out of sight!

Illuminated Lines of the Cosmos

In galaxies far, I write my rhymes,
With quarks and pixels in silly climes.
The milky way giggles at my jest,
As I pen down dreams in a cosmic quest.

The aliens dance to my cosmic beat,
With green feet tapping, it's quite a treat.
Satellites hum my melody fine,
As I juggle stardust and moonlit wine.

Comets crash into my punchlines bright,
Shooting past laughter in the starry night.
Black holes chuckle, so hard they spin,
Entranced by the laughter that lies within.

So here in space, where joy takes flight,
My pen is a rocket, igniting the night.
In every letter, a twinkling star,
Making the universe giggle, not far.

The Soul's Interstellar Journey

A spaceship made of words takes flight,
Through wobbly orbits, all feels just right.
My soul's a sparkle in a dreamy lane,
Sending postcards from Jupiter's rain.

Venus whispers secrets in a playful tone,
While Mars sends back selfies, all alone.
Stars hold a party, they pop and fizz,
As I slip on chaos, a dazzling whiz.

With cosmic puns and planetary cheers,
I scribble laughs through the stardust years.
Galactic giggles echo near and far,
As my heart races past a supernova bazaar.

No roadmaps needed in this quirky domain,
Just follow the jesters who roam like a plane.
In each starlit corner, joy's the decree,
In this soul trip of mine, I'm forever free.

Chasing Comets with Words

I chase comets across the sky's great dome,
With a quill in hand, I feel right at home.
Slingshotting laughter through nebulae bright,
Weaving tales of mischief in the soft starlight.

With every swoosh, a word takes flight,
Oh, what a spectacle, what a sight!
I scribble quirks on meteor trails,
As cosmic laughter within me sails.

Planets play catch with asteroids round,
With echoes of humor that joyfully sound.
Galaxies twirl in a comedic spree,
As I ride stardust, wild and free.

So here I stand, a jovial bard,
In a universe vast, never feels too hard.
With comets to catch and verses to spin,
The chase of giggles is my favorite win.

Echoing Starlit Silhouettes

In the shadows where starlight gleams,
I sketch funny shapes, living my dreams.
With giggles echoing off lunar beams,
An art exhibit of cosmic memes.

Galactic shadows dance and play,
While I giggle at the nightly ballet.
Starlit outlines get tangled and wry,
As I toss my thoughts to the twinkling sky.

Each comet leaves a wink in flight,
Stitching wisecracks into the night.
With laughter stretching across time and space,
Reflections of joy in this vast embrace.

So as the universe wraps me tight,
I draw starlit giggles with sheer delight.
In every silhouette, a story awaits,
A playful journey through the heavens' gates.

Letters to a Celestial Lover

Oh starry darling up so high,
Can we meet near the comet's fly?
I sent my heart through a black hole,
But it bounced back, just like my soul.

Your laughter echoes in the void,
Each giggle makes the stardust joyed.
I wrote you poems on a Moonbeam,
But the paper's stuck—what a silly theme!

Dancing moons in a waltz so fine,
I'm sending hugs through the space-time line.
Your smile lights up the asteroid belt,
Kinda like the nachos that I once felt.

So let's trade stars, my cosmic mate,
And moonwalk on the rings of fate.
I'll bring the snacks from Mars's store,
Together we'll laugh and explore some more.

Verses in the Language of Light

In cosmic tongues, we sing and play,
Flashing ideas like light years away.
With photons dancing in vibrant hues,
I'll braid your halo with purple muse.

Quasars giggle, they know our tune,
While planets twirl beneath the Moon.
I'll throw a party on that big ol' star,
Invite the sun, but maybe not Mars.

We'll toast to time with a jolt of fun,
And watch the stars (sorry, not the sun!).
With rhymes like comets, we'll zoom around,
Crafting verses from cosmic sound.

So dear light, let's brighten the night,
With silly words that take flight.
We'll scribble joy in starlit ink,
And laugh until we can't even think.

Poetic Adventures Across the Cosmos

Zooming past on this rocket ride,
With cookies baking and dreams worldwide.
We'll surf the rings of Saturn's show,
And sing flat notes—a galactic flow!

Pulsars blink like disco balls,
Inviting us to dance in cosmic halls.
Watch out, there's a meteor shower—
But all we want is a lunar flower!

In every corner, wonders compile,
With alien buddies who laugh and smile.
Together we'll scribble on Martian sand,
Sharing secrets across the land.

With each adventure, let's spread good cheer,
For stars make great friends, it's perfectly clear!
So grab your pen and let's explore,
The universe is large, and we want more!

Echoing Ballads of the Night Sky

Up in the night where the giggles ring,
We'll serenade Mercury with a funny fling.
Singing to Saturn, oh what a sight,
With shimmering moons that twinkle so bright.

Let's challenge Orion to an arm wrestling match,
And if he loses, we'll call it a hatch.
The Big Dipper offers fries with a shake,
Let's dine on stardust, what a chance to take!

With each strum of the cosmic guitar,
We'll travel through time—from near and far.
So if you hear laughter in the night,
Just know we're jamming with pure delight!

So lift your voice, let the cosmos hum,
For the universe is our stage—let's come!
With echoes of joy that never cease,
Let's dance through the stars, and feel the peace.

Quasar Quintets

A quasar quipped with a starry wink,
"My light's so fast, it makes time sink!"
While planets giggled in cosmic delight,
Playing catch with a comet in flight.

A meteor strolled like it owned the sky,
Its tail a feather, oh so spry!
"Catch me if you can," it taunted the moon,
Dancing 'round asteroids, a silly cartoon.

Stars wore hats like they were in a show,
With bright little bows and a cosmic glow.
Galaxies twirled in a waltz so grand,
While black holes snickered, "Ain't it all planned?"

Space dust gathered for a talent night,
With supernovae buzzing, oh what a sight!
As galaxies laughed, on Old Neptune's throne,
They toasted to dreams in the great unknown.

Starlit Refrains

In a nebula's cradle, the snickers arise,
Where stardust plays tricks with glimmering eyes.
Asteroids chuckled, chasing a rhyme,
While Saturn giggled at the passage of time.

A shooting star poofed, then forgot how to fly,
Swirled in its thoughts, it just floated by.
"What's the rush?" it cheerfully said,
"Life's just a ride, on this cosmic bed!"

Comets wore sunglasses, sipping on light,
Daring each other to zoom through the night.
While little green aliens, in laughter, confessed,
"We dance with the planets, we're truly blessed!"

Galaxies spun tales of cosmic glee,
Where every black hole just sat down for tea.
In this radiant quilt of a starry parade,
The universe chuckled, never afraid.

Poems of Pulsars and Planets

Pulsars pulsed out a rhythmic beat,
With planets joining in on funky feet.
"Do the worm!" cried Venus, with a wink and a grin,
While Jupiter's storms spun the dance floor in.

Mars brought snacks, from craters it found,
While little moons played tag all around.
"Who's it?" they shrieked, with a gleeful cheer,
As light-years giggled, increasing their sphere.

A rogue planet wandered, lost but not blue,
"I'm just here to party," it laughed, "Who are you?"
Stars sparkled brighter in the cosmic embrace,
As all shared a joke in this vast, merry space.

Supernovae sprinkled confetti of light,
Setting the stage for a galactic night.
With laughter and joy beaming all through,
In this swirling dance, every moment felt new.

In the Orbit of Imagination

In a swirl of colors, ideas took flight,
Planets imagined their own disco night.
Uranus boogied, sporting a crown,
While Neptune spun freely, never a frown.

Galactic giggles echoed wide and far,
As stars swapped stories of who loved what star.
"I wrote a poem to you!" said a shy little sun,
"Your warmth inspired me, isn't that fun?"

Moons made of cheese rolled down the lane,
With comet-powered cars, they raced just the same.
"Life in the void can be quite absurd,"
Chortled a black hole, single-chorded and blurred.

Through the expanse, where imagination thrives,
Laughter drifts gently, the soul it revives.
In this vast playground where dreams intertwine,
We find our joy, lost in cosmic design.

Rhymes of the Celestial Sea

In a rocket that zoomed past the moon,
I found a green alien humming a tune.
He danced with a cat that wore a top hat,
And served me a snack made of cheese and a rat.

Stars twinkled and giggled in cosmic delight,
As we played hopscotch with comets at night.
He told me jokes of a starfish named Lou,
Who proposed to a planet, but it said, "Not you!"

Flipping through galaxies, we showed off our flair,
Pretending to juggle with asteroids in the air.
But oh, what a mess when one fell on my shoe!
The aliens laughed, saying, "Now you're in the crew!"

So if you gaze up at the night sky so wide,
Remember the giggles and universal pride.
For out there, you'll find, it's a whimsical spree,
In the rhymes of the ocean of dreams wild and free.

Galactic Echoes in Starlit Silence

In a nebula, two robots had a chat,
One liked to dance, the other to chat.
They waltzed on a comet while eating some pie,
Singing to planets that spun quickly by.

A wormhole opened, and in came a clown,
With a purple spaceship and bright, silly gown.
He juggled black holes, one slipped through his hand,
And caused a big vortex that swallowed a band!

They played jazzy music from deep in the space,
While stars clapped their twinkles with infinite grace.
A supernova burst; it lit up the night,
As everyone laughed at the comic delight.

So come join the fun where the galaxies roam,
With laughter and joy as we all find a home.
For in the vastness, humor we'll trace,
Creating our echoes in this starlit space.

Verses from the Cosmic Abyss

In the depths of the void, I found a nice snack,
A sandwich that giggled and asked, "Want a whack?"
The bread was a planet, the lettuce a star,
And mayo was stardust, oh, how bizarre!

Nearby, a meteor played tic-tac-toe,
With a bubbling gas giant, just putting on a show.
"I win!" said the meteor, then did a cartwheel,
While asteroids cheered; it was quite the big deal!

A starling flew by with a name tag that read,
"I'm here for the puns, and the sky's my bread!"
We told cosmic jokes till our sides they did ache,
One about a black hole that couldn't get a break.

So if you're ever lost in the cosmic abyss,
Remember the laughter, the joy, and the bliss.
For amongst the dark voids, there's humor to find,
In the verses of stardust, where giggles unwind.

Nebulae of Words Unfurled

A colorful nebula greeted me with a grin,
It winked like a cat, then spun round with a spin.
"I rhyme for the stars, and I dance for the moon,
In cosmic poetry, we all find our tune!"

With asteroids marching in perfect parade,
They whispered to planets; it was quite a charade.
A comet threw confetti, it sparkled so bright,
While satellites giggled, sharing jokes in the night.

A galaxy swayed to a tune from afar,
While aliens played kazoo in a sparkling car.
They sang of the wonders, of how we are free,
In the nebulae of laughter, of joy, and esprit!

So if wanderers seek tales of humor unfurled,
Just look to the skies, let your laughter be twirled.
For amongst the vast cosmos, there's joy to behold,
In the words of the universe, fun stories retold.

Galactic Whispers of the Heart

In a spaceship made of cheese,
Asteroids dance with such ease.
A comet sneezes, what a sight!
Stars twinkle at the thrill of night.

Alien poets scribble in space,
With pens made of a fishy embrace.
Their lines ripple, like wormholes wide,
Spreading laughter with every glide.

Planets hold contests for the best rhyme,
Jupiter chuckles, 'I'm short on time!'
While Saturn spins rings of pure jest,
In this galaxy, humor's the quest.

So grab a star, and write away,
Join cosmic quips that brighten the day.
With giggles echoing through the void,
In this universe, joy is enjoyed!

Cosmic Lore and Lunar Legends

In the shadows of a quirky moon,
Space squirrels conduct a jovial tune.
They gather stardust for fancy pies,
Feeding rockets with laughter-filled skies.

A Martian crafts tales of silly fate,
With plot twists that could not wait.
His audience, a crowd of stars,
All chuckling from afar in their cars.

Jokes land like meteors in a line,
As orbits wobble, laughter is divine.
Each punchline lights a galaxy bright,
Drawing smiles from the dark of night.

So write your words on cosmic beams,
Let your heart soar, let it dream.
For in this expanse of whimsical lore,
Every giggle opens a door!

Between Nova and Black Hole

In the dance between light and shade,
A black hole wonders, 'Am I being played?'
While novas burst, spreading joy so grand,
Leaving cosmic laughter across the land.

Stardust junkies trade jokes in the breeze,
Even gravity can't silence their tease.
Quasars winking, with a twinkly flair,
Shooting satirical beams through cosmic air.

Galaxies giggle, colliding with cheer,
Creating comedy, year after year.
And through the void, echoes of glee,
Resound in the heart of eternity.

So float on a comet, let humor unfold,
From the wonders of space to the stories told.
For every twinkling star will proclaim,
That laughter across light years is the name of the game!

Starbound Stories of the Heart

Beneath the nebula's playful glow,
Constellations giggle, moving slow.
Each star tells a tale of whimsical dreams,
In a universe stitched with laughter's seams.

Black cats in space wearing hats so bold,
Plotting mischief, or so I'm told.
They chase shooting stars, dodging the rays,
With their laughter echoing through all the ways.

Supernova parties, everyone's invited,
Cake baked from stardust, delight ignited.
With frolicking comets and meteor showers,
Funny fables bloom like galactic flowers.

So pen your heart under cosmic lights,
Wait for the humor that daily ignites.
For between the stars, joy is the art,
Forever spinning with stories to chart!

www.ingramcontent.com/pod-product-compliance
Lightning Source LLC
Chambersburg PA
CBHW071826160426
43209CB00003B/211